Getting to Know & Love Islam

A CHILDREN'S BOOK INTRODUCING THE RELIGION OF ISLAM

BY THE SINCERE SEEKER KIDS COLLECTION

What is Islam?

Islam is to obey and submit fully to our Creator, the Creator of you and me, the Creator of this whole world and everything around us. We can only live peacefully and happily in this world and the next when we submit to God by believing in Him and obeying His commands.

Islam is a religion in which Muslims believe and worship the One True God, Allah, who knows everything and is All-Powerful and All-Loving. He loves us very much, and we should love him too.

Islam is a complete way of life that teaches us how to live and what teaches us what is good and bad. Following Islam will make us better human beings.

Allah created us so we can worship Him and test us. Islam teaches us to be good to our parents, friends, and neighbors and help those in need. If we believe in God and live a good life, we will be rewarded with Paradise in the afterlife, where we will live there forever and can wish for anything we want.

Who is Allah?

The word *Allah* is the name of God. He is the One and Only God. Allah never had a beginning and was never born. Allah will never have an end. He is the Creator of the Heavens and Earth, the Creator of the Universe, the Creator of you and me. Everything belongs to Allah. He is the King of all kings. Allah has no father, mother, son, daughter, family, or equal. Nothing is like Allah. Our minds cannot imagine how he looks. Allah does not get tired, He does not rest, and He does not sleep.

Allah knows everything. Allah sees and hears everything. Allah is the One that provides us with many delicious foods, tasty drinks, and a comfortable home. He is the One that sends us rain, shines the bright sun, and lights the beautiful big moon. He is the One that gifted us our lives, our loving parents, and our happy families. He gifted us the ability to hear, feel, taste, and see. God gifted us with our hearts, minds, souls, strengths, and skills. Allah gives and gives and gives.

Allah is the Most Loving, Most Merciful, and Most Forgiving. Allah deserves to be worshipped and obeyed. God is the One that takes care of us, protects us, and loves us so much. We should turn to Allah when having a bad day and thank Him when we are having a good day. We should talk and make dua and prayers to Allah and ask him for everything because He owns everything. He is always listening and can hear everything we say and ask. He knows every secret. We should turn to Allah for answers, help, and protection too. When we make a mistake, we ask Allah to forgive us, and He will accept it and forgive us.

Allah is above us, above the Heavens, above his throne. Allah has many names - 99 special names. We should memorize them to learn more about and get closer to Him. Allah should be our best friend. He knows and loves us so much; we should get to know and love him back.

What is the Holy Quran?

Allah talks to us and tells us what we should and should not do in His Book, the Holy Quran. The word Quran means *recitation*. Allah sent down the Holy Quran with Angel Gabriel, who recited it to Prophet Muhammad, peace be upon him, who then recited it to us. The Holy Quran was revealed in the Holy Month of Ramadan, the 9th month of the Islamic calendar. The Holy Quran contains the exact words of Allah, word by word, letter by letter. The Holy Quran has never been changed. The Holy Quran is written in the Arabic language.

The Holy Quran is a guide on how we should live our lives. The Holy Quran teaches us that we should be truthful and never lie or cheat, give charity to the poor, and be kind and just to our parents, neighbors, family, and friends. The Holy Quran warns us about mistreating people, animals, and plants. The Holy Quran teaches us to love, compassion, faith, and goodwill. Allah reminds us of His love, compassion, and mercy throughout the Holy Quran. If we follow the Holy Quran, we will live a good life in this world and be rewarded with Paradise in the afterlife.

The Holy Quran is memorized by millions of people of all ages from all over the world. It is the most read Book in the world. Allah made a promise in the Holy Quran to make it easy for people to understand and memorize it. The Holy Quran is meant to be read in a beautiful melodic tone. The Holy Quran has 114 chapters called Surah in Arabic, and each sentence or phrase is called an Ayat. The Holy Quran is God's biggest miracle and contains hundreds of miracles. We should read the Holy Quran daily and learn its powerful lessons.

Who are Messengers and Prophets of God?

God, the Almighty, chose Messengers and Prophets to deliver His message and teach us what He wants and expects from us. God has sent thousands of Prophets and Messengers to us throughout history. Every nation on Earth has received a Messenger or Prophet. All the Messengers and Prophets of God taught the same general message that no one is worthy of worship except Allah, and He is the One and Only, without any partners, son, daughter, or equal. All other gods are false and are only creations of God, not the actual Creator. Listening to Allah's Messengers and Prophets and obeying them would lead us to build a relationship with Allah and love Him.

Muslims believe, respect, honor, and love all Messengers and Prophets of God, starting with Prophet Adam, including Noah, Abraham, Ishmael, Jacob, Moses, and Prophet Jesus, peace be upon them all. God chose the best among us to deliver His message. The Prophets and Messengers were the best in morals and manners. The last and final Messenger and Prophet of God is Prophet Muhammad, peace be upon him, who was sent to the last and final nation, our nation.

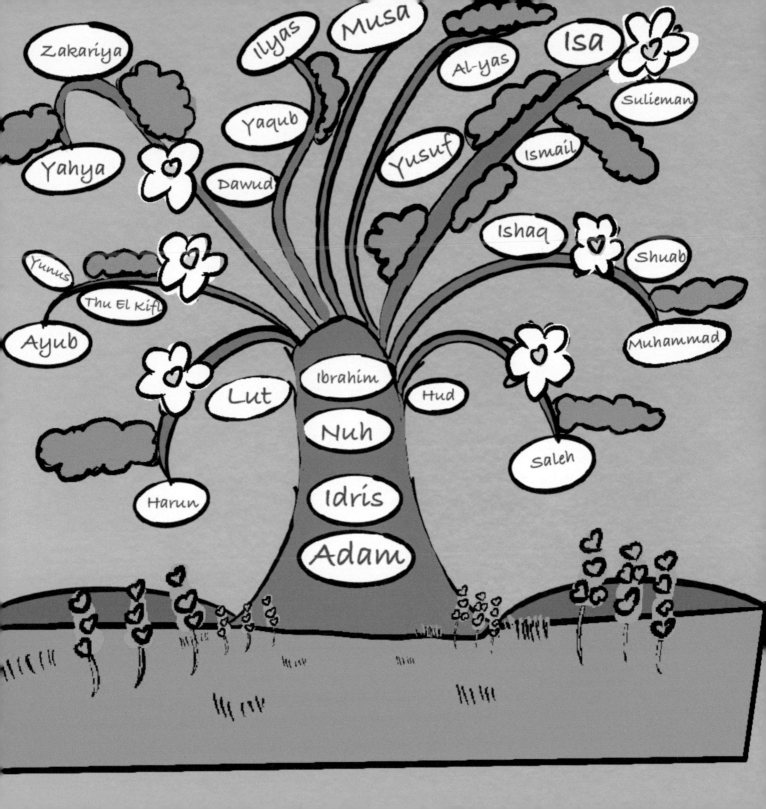

Who Were the Past Nations & What Happened to Them?

God's Prophets came with miracles and signs to prove God sent them. Only Prophets can perform miracles. God provided Prophet Moses, peace be upon him, miracles, such as the power to turn his stick into a snake and to split the Red Sea. These miracles were to humble and remind people that God's power, control, and might is true. Prophet Jesus, peace be upon him, had a miraculous birth without a father and was able to heal sick people with leprosy, cure the blind, and resurrect the dead, all with the permission and will of God. The last and final Prophet of God, Muhammad, peace be upon him, was provided a miracle that we can all see and hear today, the Holy Quran, which contains hundreds of miracles.

The Holy Quran talks about stories of previous nations, where Messengers and the Prophet were sent down to deliver God's message. But the people rejected, disobeyed, and denied God's message. God sent Prophet Noah, peace be upon him, to his people, where he preached the message of Allah for 950 years, calling people to worship the One God and follow his commandments, but only a few people believed in him. His people denied and made fun of him. After the denial, God instructed Prophet Noah, peace be upon him, to build a ship. His people thought he was crazy for making a boat on land without water nearby.

God instructed Prophet Noah to enter the ship with those who believed in His Message. He also asked Prophet Noah to take a male and female of every animal aboard. Soon, water started to come out from the Earth and fall from the sky. Then God caused a great flood; the water came out from every crack on the Earth, and rain fell from the skies like never before. Then the flood washed out the evil people.

Who is Prophet Muhammad PBUH?

Before Prophet Muhammad, peace be upon him, Prophets were only sent to specific people in specific places and periods. However, Prophet Muhammad PBUH is the last and final Prophet, meant for all humankind until the end of time.

Prophet Muhammad, peace be upon him, was born in Mecca, in the Arabian Peninsula. The people of Mecca were devoted idol worshippers and the area and period at the time were full of ignorance, foolishness, and misguidance. At forty, Prophet Muhammad received his first Revelation in a cave from God through Angel Gabriel. He spent the rest of his life explaining and living the teachings of the Holy Qur'an and Islam, the religion that God revealed to him.

Even though he was known among his community as *the truthful the trustworthy,* most of his people did not believe him or his message. Soon after, the people who believed in the message were poorly treated by those who did not believe in the Message of God. Prophet Muhammad, peace be upon him, spread the Message of God in the city of Mecca for thirteen years. Then Prophet Muhamad PBUH and the believers migrated to the city of Medina, where he gained many more followers, who made him the city's leader.

The disbelievers of Mecca planned and tried to attack Islam and the Muslims, but what was originally a small group of Muslims grew in number, and they survived the attack of the disbelievers. The Prophet led an army back to Mecca within ten years and conquered Mecca. Later, Islam spread throughout the World. Prophet Muhammad PBUH died in 632. God states in the Holy Quran that He did not send Prophet Muhammad, peace be upon him, except as a mercy for us.

Prophet Muhammad, peace be upon him, was sent to guide and lead us to Allah. Prophet Muhammad, peace be upon him, understood the Holy Quran. He loved the Holy Quran and lived his life based on its teachings. He is the best role model for us. He is the one with outstanding virtues and characteristics. He was the best husband, father, grandfather, leader, teacher, judge, and statesman. He preached justice, fairness, peace, and love.

Muslims try to copy and follow Prophet Muhammad's faith, behavior, attitude, patience, compassion, and righteousness. We try to copy the way the Prophet ate, drank, the position he slept in, and the way he behaved and interacted with others. The act of copying the Prophet is called Sunnah.

What is a Muslim?

The word *Muslim* means someone submitting to Allah's will and laws. The message of Islam has always been meant for all people. Anyone who accepts this message becomes a Muslim. One out of four persons on this Earth is a Muslim. There are 1.8 billion Muslims, about 24% of the world's population. Only 18% of Muslims are Arabs. Many Muslims live in Europe, South East Asia, & the West. Islam is not limited to one ethnicity or group of people. Muslims come from various ethnic backgrounds, races, cultures, and national origins.

In Islam, worshipping God includes every act, belief, or statement which God approves and loves. Anything that brings a person closer to Allah is an act of worship. Worshipping Allah includes the daily ritual prayers, fasting, charity, and even believing in the Angels, God's books, and His Prophets. Worshipping God also includes loving God, being thankful to Him, and placing your trust in Him.

What is the Purpose of Our Life?

We cannot know the purpose of our life unless God guides us. We must ask our Creator for guidance, to show us the straight path and teach us why we were created. God guides us through His book, the Holy Quran, and prayers. Our goal is to become a believer in Him and a good servant by obeying Him. Those who pass this test will enter Paradise forever. The purpose of our life is to find Allah, build a relationship with Him, and try our best to obey His commands and be the best person we can be. Life in this world is also a test for us. God is testing all of us. If we live a good life as Muslims, we pass the test.

What is Hadith & Sunnah?

The Holy Quran is the primary Source of Islam and the literal Spoken Word of God. The Holy Quran is the only Book in the world with God's exact and pure word. Meanwhile, Hadith is the second source of Islam. Unlike the Holy Quran, the statements known as Hadith were preserved by humans and not directly by God.

While Prophet Muhammad, peace be upon him, was practicing and preaching the teachings of Islam and the Holy Quran to his companions, his companions would report and record the statements, actions, and beliefs of the Prophet. The companions of Prophet Muhammad, peace be upon him, gathered them, and later, scholars who specialized in Hadith collected these reports.

Hadith refers to a narration or report that Prophet Muhammad, peace be upon him, said, did, or approved. Hadith can also refer to the Prophet's reaction, or silence in response to something said or done by others.

The acts and practices of the Prophet are called Sunnah. Prophet Muhammad PBUH stands as the sacred model to copy and follow, as God sent him to us as an example of how we should live our lives.

What are the Six Articles of Faith?

To become a Muslim, each follower must believe in six Articles of Faith (which translates to the word *Iman* in Arabic). These six articles of Faith form the foundation of the Islamic belief system.

Belief in the Oneness of Allah
Belief in the Angels of Allah
Belief in the Prophets and Messengers of Allah
Belief in the Books of Allah
Belief in the Last Day and Resurrection Day, and Judgement Day
Belief in Divine Predestination

Oneness of God

The first and most important article of faith in Islam is the belief in the Oneness of God. Faith begins with believing in Allah, the Glorious, from which all other facets of faith spring. A Muslim believes and acknowledges that no one is worthy of their worship, love, loyalty, sacrifice, hope, and fear other than Allah, our Creator. God does not like it when people worship other gods because all other gods are false. God is the Only One to whom worship is due.

What are the Five Pillars of Islam?

The Religion of Islam is based on Five Primary Foundations or Pillars. These Five Pillars or religious duties are required, and every Muslim must follow and practice them to the best of their ability. The Five Pillars are mentioned individually throughout the Holy Quran, and through narrations of Prophet Muhammad, peace be upon him. The Five Pillars of Islam are:

Testimony of faith in the Oneness of God (Allah) and the last and final Prophet, Muhammad, peace be upon him.
Establishment of the Five Mandatory Prayers
Concern and almsgiving to the needy (Zakat in Arabic)
Fasting during the month of Ramadan (for Self-purification)
The Pilgrimage to Makkah (at least once in a lifetime for those who can perform it and can afford it)

Muslims take these five pillars very seriously and prioritize them over all other things in life.

What is Jannah (Paradise)?

Jannah is often translated as *Green Garden*. Jannah or Paradise is located in the Seventh Heaven. All Muslims must believe in Jannah (Paradise). It is a beautiful, relaxing, peaceful, fun place where Muslims who believe in God and live a good life will live forever. Whatever someone wishes for in Jannah, they will get. The people of Jannah will only see good things and listen to beautiful sounds. The people of Jannah will be with other good people and reunite with righteous family members. There is no sadness, pain, worries, boredom, anger, hate, jealousy, sickness, or fear in Jannah.

Jannah is so big and beautiful that our minds cannot even imagine it. Paradise has seven levels, and each has many stages and categories. Each level in Paradise has greater joys and pleasures and is more amazing than the one under it. Paradise has Eight Gates. The highest level of Paradise is called *Jannat Ul-Firdous*.

Paradise will have many mansions, all made of gold on top of silver. There will be rooms upon rooms inside these palaces with waterfalls falling beneath them. The Soil of Jannah is made of pure white musk, and the pebbles are made of pearls, rubies, diamonds, and jewels. The people of Jannah will lean back in their luxurious high, soft couches and beds with cup holders and comfortable blankets. The dwellers of Paradise will eat and drink whatever they wish. If one sees a bird he wishes to eat, it would fall roasted between his hands. Cups will be served to them with shiny rubies, pearls, and diamonds. Fruits will hang freely from trees and are automatically lowered for them to enjoy. The clothes of Jannah will never wear out of age.

Nothing will be more beloved and enjoyable than the best gift in Paradise: seeing the face of Allah, the Glorious. This is the most precious gift to those who live a good life. We should try our best to live good lives so we can enter Paradise with our families and live happily ever after.

The End.

Printed in France by Amazon
Brétigny-sur-Orge, FR

18753622R00018